LESSONS
LEARNED

FRANK A. SILANE

JULY 31, 2020

READ THIS FIRST!

When I started on this project, I struggled to decide on a title. I decided on "Lessons Learned" because it best describes what I have set out to pass on—a lifetime of lessons that I have learned from my personal observations, from what I have learned from experience. The information which follows is a collection and summary of what I believe works best for a happy and successful life and what does not.

The title "Lessons Learned" underscores two essential points. The first is that this is *not* information which I have authored. Instead, it summarizes what I have learned from others and what I have gleaned from experience.

Secondly, and this is important, I do *not* hold myself out as an example or model of the principles which I have described in the following pages. To the contrary, I have often fallen short of my own standards or failed to follow my own guidelines, but I have learned more from my failures than from my successes. What is important is that, when you do fail, as you will, you do not blame or change the standards. You do not quit. You recognize your shortcomings, you learn from them, and you improve.

As I started to write this book, I reflected on the fact that, at the end of my career, I was much more competent than when I started. As a new lawyer, I had the same natural abilities and limitations as I did when retired. Yet, when I retired, I was much more equipped to deal with whatever issues came my way. I didn't get smarter in the intervening years. The difference, of course, is having years of experience observing successes and failures, good relationships and bad, and what it takes to succeed in the right way.

Life experience is like playing a videogame. No matter how skilled you are, you perform better the second or third time through because you learn from your mistakes. You learn what works and where the pitfalls are. You can learn from someone who has played the game and who can tell you where the pitfalls are.

That is essentially the thought process which motivated me to put my thoughts on paper. I have been very fortunate to have lived long enough, and had a varied life and career, which allowed me to observe successes and failures, good leadership and bad, happy lives and tragedies. If you live long enough and pay attention, you should learn something about how to live. It would be a waste not to pass those acquired observations to people who have not yet fully "played the game."

DEDICATION

I have been blessed in life beyond measure with great parents, wife, children, grandchildren, extended family, friends, law partners, and employees, all of whom have contributed to my life. There are two who are particularly relevant to this book:

Roy Silane: My father. He had a wealth of homespun philosophy and wisdom that made a positive difference in my life and in the lives of so many others, well beyond our immediate family. Always positive, always unselfish, always caring and, in his way, a natural leader.

Barbara Silane "Nonns": As I completed writing about the positive values in this book it occurred to me that no one exemplifies many of those qualities more than Barbara. In her own quiet way she is a true example of what it takes to lead a productive and truly valuable life--- and my life has been enriched immeasurably because of it.

INDEX

BELIEVE IN YOURSELF

If you don't believe in yourself, no one will believe in you.

When I began to assemble these notes, I had to decide which topic had the broadest significance for all the topics to follow and for life in general. The choice was obvious: personal self–confidence and the related and more important topic of being comfortable with yourself.

Self-confidence and being comfortable with yourself are the true keys to success in life, to strong personal relationships and to personal peace of mind. Lack of self-confidence and being insecure leads to stress, frustration, and can sometimes strain personal relationships.

"Self-confidence" is difficult to define. It helps to understand what "self-confidence" is *not*.

Self-confidence is *not* arrogance. It is *not* the belief that you are as talented or as qualified as others. There will always be someone smarter, bigger, stronger, better looking etc.

Self-confidence is *not* the foolish belief that you can be the best, or even good at, anything that you try to do. (No matter how self-confident I am, I will never play centerfield for the Yankees).

Self-confidence is *not* the absence of all self-doubt or personal insecurity. Anyone smart enough to have self-awareness has some level of self-doubt and insecurity -- some just hide it better than others. A healthy dose of doubt and insecurity means that you are smart enough to know your limitations. A healthy dose of self-doubt provides the incentive to overcome your weaknesses and to improve as a person. Most highly successful people have had to overcome self-doubt, personal limitations, and failures.

So what is self-confidence? Self-confidence is being comfortable with who you are, as you are. It is believing in yourself and being comfortable with your own unique combination of talents, qualities, *and* with your own limitations. It is being comfortable in your own skin, *without* measuring yourself against others. It is being able to lead your own life, following your own course, without being concerned with what other people are doing. If you can achieve that, many of life's challenges fall more easily into place.

It is both frustrating and counter-productive to measure yourself against others. No two people are the same. No two people have the same unique set of abilities and limitations.

People tend to be judged, at least initially, on the qualities that can be seen or measured. People are rarely measured on the important intangibles that are not always obvious and that make each of us who we are. For example, we commonly refer to a person's academic record, and the reputation of the schools attended, as a measure of a person's overall ability to achieve. Academic excellence is certainly a valuable piece of information to consider. But it is only a piece, and not the most important piece. Academic excellence does not always equate to success in life. There are countless instances of people with excellent academic credentials who are failures in life. I have worked with people with the best academic records from the best schools in the world but whose professional talents were quite limited because they lacked the important intangibles.

The reverse is equally true. There are countless examples

of highly talented and successful people who were overlooked because they fell short of the objective criteria commonly, and necessarily, relied on by those doing the recruiting.

The world of sports is replete with examples which demonstrate that observable standards are very limited predictors of success. Like the academic world, the world of sports relies heavily on certain measurable or observable criteria to evaluate a developing athlete. Scouts in every sport look at accepted criteria for the size, speed, leaping ability etc., of an athlete. They look at the school that the athlete attended. Yet many of the very greatest athletes were overlooked because they did not fit the "measurable" objective criteria normally considered by coaches and scouts. Many were overlooked or underestimated early in their careers because they were too small, too slow, went to the wrong schools, etc. They went on to be "greats" because they possessed personal qualities which are not easy to see and which cannot be measured—and, most importantly, they *believed in themselves* even with their limitations. The same is true in life.

As a life-long sports fan, excuse me for using a couple of sports references. The examples apply equally to all aspects of life. Here are two examples that resonate with me.

Jose Altuve, second basemen for the Houston Astro's exemplifies the principle. At a time when professional athletes are getting bigger and stronger and being measured, among other things, by their physical dimensions, Jose Altuve is the shortest player in professional baseball. What is instructive is how he got there and what he did with the opportunity. He is from Venezuela. Being generous, he is five feet six inches tall.

As a teenager he showed up for a tryout at an Astros camp but was sent home because he was "too small." He returned the next day, uninvited, and convinced the scouts to look at him. He did not let his limitations define him. He has since become among the best players in a generation, a regular all-star selection, a batting champion, league MVP, World Series MVP, etc., etc. He succeeded because he believed in himself and believed "I can" rather than "I can't." He would not allow himself to be a victim of other people's standards. It is true that he had to do more than others to prove himself but he didn't use his size as an excuse. He believed in himself and he overcame. He had the intangibles that don't show up on paper.

One more example—also from the world of sports: I recently heard an interview with Gerald McCoy, all pro defensive tackle with the Dallas Cowboys. He was being interviewed from his home and behind him was a poster of Batman. When asked about his favorite superhero he explained why he chose Batman. His answer was both instructive and intelligent. Superman, he said, was born with all sorts of powers, Batman was not. Batman had to work, to focus, to learn, to be disciplined. McCoy said that Batman defined him because he was not born with outstanding physical qualities. He did not excel in any of the usual measurable criteria used by recruiters. Others were bigger, faster etc., but he was focused, disciplined, and motivated. He did better because he believed and he used his personal intangibles to overcome and excel.

I use these examples from the world of sports because they present such clear examples. But the same principles apply everywhere in life. There is no objective measure of the qualities that make people happy and successful. There is no objective measure of determination, reliability, loyalty, focus, discipline, and diligence. There is no objective measure of one's ability to take on responsibility, to motivate others, and to lead. There is no objective measure of common sense. Most importantly, there is no objective measure of the totality of everything that makes you who you are. *The ultimate measure of success is the way you lead your life, and that takes time and it takes patience.*

This is not an easy lesson to learn. It is difficult to understand and accept as a child, perhaps even more so in your teens and even into early adulthood. Others often seem to be more talented, more popular, or more self-assured. Sometimes others may seem to be moving ahead with opportunities, when we are not. The talents and the successes of others shouldn't matter to you. You should applaud the successes of others. What matters in your life is what *you* do with *your* talents. *No one on this planet has your unique set of talents.* If you work comfortably, diligently—and patiently--within your own unique set of skills and limitations, without looking to the sides to see what others are doing, you will be surprised to see how, over time, you will overcome the obstacles and you will succeed. You will be surprised to see how many of those who seem to have had an edge, have fallen by the wayside while you have moved on. Just focus on your own efforts and be comfortable with who you are.

One final note, and an important one: Trusting yourself often requires a great deal of *patience*, particularly when those around you may seem to be progressing faster. And patience can be difficult to have, especially when you are young. Life is a marathon and not a sprint. The "winners" in life are generally those who maintain and practice the right values, consistently and reliably, over the long term. It may take time to see the results of your efforts, but if you keep faith with yourself and maintain your personal standards, the results will follow.

THE IMPORTANCE OF YOUR WORD

It does not require many words to speak the truth.

Chief Joseph (Chief, Nez Perce)

When I started to write on this topic I intended to combine it with the related topic of personal integrity. After giving it some thought, I decided to treat the topics separately because, even though your word and your personal integrity are related, they are not necessarily coextensive. A person may have personal integrity even though his or her word may not be entirely reliable for any number of perfectly innocent reasons having nothing to do with the person's integrity.

Here, my goal is to emphasize the importance of disciplining yourself to make your word as truthful and as reliable as possible. Your word should not be gold, it should be platinum. Like it or not, you will be defined, to some degree, by the value of your word. Ultimately, your friends and your peers will, consciously or unconsciously, consider your personal credibility as a measure of who you are.

Anyone who has worked with me has heard me say, repeatedly, in a professional context: "Never lose your credibility." It is a valuable principle. It requires more than fundamental honesty. It requires self-awareness and discipline.

Here are a few thoughts which may help to establish and maintain your credibility:

1. *Be reliable: Do what you say you are going to do—even in small things:*

   There is an old adage: *"Your word is you bond."* The Merriam-Webster dictionary defines the "bond," in this context, as *"a binding agreement—a Covenant"* The old adage is correct: When you give your word, it should be like a binding agreement, something on which people can rely.

   Friends and colleagues should be able to say with confidence: *"If _____ says he/she will be there, he/she will be there."* Whenever you say you will do something, even casually, make sure that you do it. Conversely, don't say you will do something if there is a doubt that you can or will follow through. If you have some doubt about whether you can or will follow through, say that when you make the commitment. If you do make a commitment, even a small one, and you change your mind or can't follow through, let the other person know. Let them know that when you say something, they can count on it. Maintain your credibility! It will define who you are.

2. *Be accurate: Make sure that information that you give others is accurate. Where there is a level of uncertainty, explain the level of your belief in its accuracy.*

   Don't provide information as an absolute truth unless you are personally sure it is true. If you just believe the information is true, qualify it by explaining the basis for your belief. *i.e., "I have not confirmed [----] but I believe it to be true"* or *"I have heard from people that I trust..."*

I sometimes use a personal gimmick to explain my personal level of belief. I sometimes use the ten point scale. When trying to recall a fact or relay information, I will often say: *"On a scale of one to ten, I will give my level of confidence a six" (or less than five if I have serious doubt.)* The gimmick is not for everyone, but it makes the point that we can try to explain how much (or how little) faith we have in the information that we pass along. It avoids looking foolish and damaging your credibility for publishing information that turns out to be wrong. Try not to be "sure" unless you are really sure!

3. *Speak your mind—respectfully: Don't fall into the trap of telling people what they want to hear:*

It is common, in a social setting, for well-intended honest people to avoid disagreeing when someone expresses a point of view or information with which they privately disagree. That is simply courtesy. Honesty does not require us to disclose everything we know or to dispute every fact or point of view with which we disagree. In fact, basic courtesy and respect for others often requires that we keep our views to ourselves if, to do otherwise, would cause unnecessary offence or embarrassment.

When your point of view really matters, speak your mind—respectfully but clearly and directly.

How do you distinguish? It is often not easy to decide when you should express your views directly and when you should withhold them. It requires judgement and common sense. Here are some situations in which you should express your views clearly, without "sugar coating":

- Know your audience. Don't give "soft" or evasive answers to people who are close to you or who expect you to give them the unvarnished truth. To do otherwise, can cause offence.

- Be clear and direct with your views when you have responsibility for others.

- State your views clearly when they may influence the outcome of any important issue.

Personally, I gravitate toward people who let me know what they think, provided they do it in good faith and with respect. I have a hard time trusting anyone who always seems to agree with my point of view. That is just not realistic, it is not credible, it is patronizing, and it is difficult to trust.

Professionally, I always welcomed disagreement and debate both on legal issues and on any other issue affecting our office operation. The reason is simple. We paid people to think. If everyone thought like me, we wouldn't need to pay for other minds-- and no one gets it right all the time.

4. *Never defend an indefensible position:*

Never try to defend a position which is wrong just because you may feel that losing a specific point will give an advantage to an opposing point of view. This is a mistake that lawyers, and others, make all the time. They fear that losing on a specific point will undermine their broader position. The reverse is actually true. When you try to defend a point which is logically or factually wrong, you risk losing credibility on everything else. If you willingly concede the points on which you are wrong, you will be more credible on the more critical points which you need to defend.

5. *Don't fight every issue:*

If you want people to listen to you, pick your fights carefully. Don't fight every issue. Don't try to dispute every apparent wrong, even when you are right. If you avoid complaining about every perceived wrong or injustice, you will earn a reputation for tolerance and reasonableness. Then, when you do speak up, people will listen. They will listen because they will know that you are not just a complainer and that the point you are making must be important.

6. *If you can't win an argument with the truth, you have the wrong side of the argument. Stated differently: Nothing works better than the truth!*

MAINTAIN YOUR INTEGRITY

STARTING NOW

More than anything else, your level of personal integrity defines who you are and how much (or how little), you are respected. More importantly, it defines how you will feel about yourself.

The Random House Dictionary defines **integrity** as: *"Adherence to moral and ethical principles; soundness of moral character; honesty."* Although that somewhat high sounding definition is accurate, it does not explain the *"moral and ethical"* principles that are a measures of a person's integrity.

Everyone may not agree on all of the traits that define integrity, but there are qualities which are universally respected. Here is a list of traits I have observed in people who have earned the respect of others. They are the traits that I instinctively admire when I see them. They are traits that we should each aspire to practice:

1. *Honesty:* I have observed that people who are consistently honest, especially when it hurts, are always respected.

2. *Being faithful to your principles:* People may disagree with you on the principles themselves, but they will always respect you for being true to your principles. This is especially true if your principles cause you to separate yourself from the crowd and to stand alone. The decision to live up to your beliefs may not be popular in the moment, but it will garner

respect in the long run, at least from the people who matter. When you compromise your personal values, for whatever reason, you lose respect from everyone, including yourself.

3. *Taking personal responsibility for your actions:* When you make a mistake, or fall short, own it. Don't make excuses. Don't blame the values. Don't blame anyone else. No one respects people who point fingers or try to shift responsibility to someone else.

4. *Forgiveness:* Take the high road. Be willing to overlook small slights and be willing to forgive wrongs when the wrongdoer is genuinely remorseful.

5. *Courage:* Have courage to follow your principles, to be honest when it is difficult to be honest, and to do what you believe to be right, even when it is not popular or easy.

6. *Be respectful to and considerate of others:* Treat everyone with genuine respect, regardless of their station in life and regardless of whether they share your views.

7. *Humility:* Being humble and modest in all that you do. Humility is worthy of respect. Let others do the bragging for you.

8. *Be of service to others:* Consider the needs and feelings of other people and, when necessary, above your own.

To reduce the list to a simple, broad statement: Be the kind of person that everyone you encounter can trust and rely on.

To be clear, no one is perfect. Few, if any, of us exhibit all of these qualities all of the time. Most of us fall short. I certainly have many times. That does not diminish the value of the message. The point is that these are timeless traits and values. They are qualities that have been respected for generations. They are qualities that we should aspire to, regardless of how many times we may fall short.

One more point: Don't confuse popularity with respect. Being popular often comes from pleasing the crowd or a group of people, regardless of whether the source of the popularity has any value. The "crowd" is, almost by definition, made up of people who are followers. Popularity is usually transient—it often doesn't last. A person can become "popular" by always being the funny guy at the party, or by being cool or charming. It says nothing about who the person is.

Integrity, is earned. It has inherent value. It produces respect which lasts, not just among followers in the crowd, but among the thinking people who lead.

As a young person it is often difficult to see what will become apparent to you later in life. Over time, many of the people who seem most popular now, will fall by the wayside. Over time, the people who live with integrity now will keep for a lifetime the respect and friendship of the people that matter most. This is not always easy to see when you are a young person in the crowd, but you will see it happen in adulthood, when it really matters.

LEADERSHIP

"People ask the difference between a leader and a boss.
The leader leads, and the boss drives."

Theodore Roosevelt

Leadership is the key to excellence in any organization
but we may not focus on what true leadership really
means. To me, leadership is the ability to motivate people
to do their very best and to be their very best. Leaders
elevate the people around them.

Many people in positions of responsibility confuse
management with leadership. They are related but
different. An organization, a group, a team, may survive
and even achieve some level of success based on
management alone but it will only reach its full potential
through effective leadership.

Management vs. Leadership

There is a fundamental difference, not often recognized,
between "leadership" and "management." The two
concepts are often confused because a person who is in a
position of authority with the power to issue orders
appears to "lead" those under his or her authority. Being
the "boss" does not make a "leader." The concept of
"leadership" is much more than simply issuing orders.

Anyone in a position of power or authority can issue
instructions and demand compliance with rules. A person
who "leads" only by asserting his or her authority can
ensure that the subordinates show up on time and work to

the letter of the organization's rules, whatever those may be. That kind of behavior does not build loyalty, does not build a team, and does not get the best that people have to offer. To the contrary, a person who deals from authority alone tends to destroy motivation and morale.

Some wise person wrote, in substance, that you can pay a person for their back but their creative side they bring as a volunteer. You cannot force a person to be enthusiastic and willing to go "above and beyond" what they are required to do simply by asserting authority and enforcing rules. You have to make them *want* to do their best. That is the mark of a true leader.

Leaders have responsibility to those they lead

The fundamental rule of leadership is respecting and caring for the people under your authority.

One noteworthy example of this kind of respect, on a corporate level, occurred a number of years ago involving Delta Airlines. Delta management was well known for being protective and caring of the needs of its employees. Delta employees were always paid and treated well. In times of recession, when traditional "business decisions" would have called for layoffs, Delta management did what it reasonably could to protect its employees and their jobs. That leadership did not go unnoticed. In 1982, airlines, including Delta, were suffering losses. Three Delta flight attendants initiated a project of donations by employees, retirees, and friends to finance the purchase of Delta's first Boeing 767 aircraft. In December of 1982, seven thousand Delta employees presented the airline with a new aircraft, aptly named "The Spirit of Delta" purchased for the airline through the spontaneous initiative of the employees. It was no surprise that Delta was widely regarded at the time as providing the best airline service in the industry. Their employees were motivated to do their best. Loyalty goes both ways, even in a corporate environment.

More recently, with the outbreak of the Covid 19 pandemic, Delta management again demonstrated its leadership by being among the first, if not the first, to forgo their salaries in an effort to protect and set an example to those for whom they were responsible.

Leadership is personal

Leadership is fundamentally personal, particularly in a smaller organization where personal contact is common and people work as a team. It is derived from mutual trust and mutual respect. That kind of personal leadership cannot be created remotely. It cannot be created through an intermediary. The leader must deal with people personally and directly, whether to acknowledge a job well done or to take corrective action where necessary.

Since this book is written primarily for my family, I will use a personal relation as an example of true personal leadership. I refer to my father. He was a sales manager in the life insurance business. He had little formal education but believed, religiously, in hard work, taking personal responsibility, and a genuine respect for anyone who did their work with pride and a smile, regardless of how exalted or menial their job might be. When they fell short, he counseled them directly.

The nature of his work required his employees to meet sales quotas which were always a challenge. Their individual income depended almost entirely on their sales production. He dramatically improved the productivity, performance, and income of many of the people who worked for him and he elevated the status of every office to which he was assigned. He achieved this using two fundamental qualities: He had, and maintained, high standards of dress and professional behavior which he applied equally to everyone regardless of status and, more importantly, he respected and genuinely cared for every employee—and they knew it.

Although it was not his job, and many would say that it was below his management position, my father would work side by side with a slumping employee, often at night, to improve the person's performance and income, turning potential failures into successes.

Instead of holding onto younger people who had leadership qualities, and who made his own job more secure, he worked to get them promoted to higher positions which caused him to lose their services. He produced more promotions of employees to positions of management than any of his contemporaries. The offices which he led were always among the most successful. His former employees never forgot how he respected them. In retirement, as an old man and infirm, he lost all his worldly possessions but his former employees never stopped caring or coming to visit. Loyalty goes both ways.

In both of these examples, the starting point is having a genuine concern for and interest in the people in your charge. It is the quality which causes others to do their best, willingly, to reach the desired result.

The principles of leadership are timeless

Don't ever succumb to the cop-out that "things are different now." Although technology and attitudes change over time, the human values that people respect most never change. The principles of true leadership never change. The qualities which make true leaders today are the same qualities practiced by Alexander the Great, Julius Caesar, and George Washington. They are *human* qualities, and they never change.

Key elements of good leadership

I have seen good leadership and bad, and the consequences of both. Here are some of the essential foundations for true leadership:

1. *Take care of your people: First and foremost, a leader must take care of the people in his or her charge.*

   If you care for your people, genuinely, they will take care of you. If the people in your charge know that you are concerned about them, ensuring that they are being treated fairly, and accommodating their legitimate personal needs where possible, they will be protective of you. This often requires putting the needs of your personnel ahead of your own immediate needs.

   In the military, a good leader will not eat unless his troops are fed and will not get his mail, or enjoy some other privilege, unless his or her troops have theirs first. In business, a leader will make sure that his or her employees are fairly compensated, and that their personal needs are observed, respected, and accommodated, where possible. The result of loyalty to your people is that they will be loyal to you.

2. *Leaders lead from the front.*

   Do not delegate tasks, then stand on the sidelines. When asking people to do demanding tasks, stay involved either directly or, if that is not practical, in spirit. Staying closely involved with the people performing the task lets them know the importance of the task and, more importantly, the importance which you place on them.

3. *Never ask anyone to do anything that you have not done or that you would not do.*

   Do not be afraid to get your hands dirty, literally or figuratively. If you lead a group of people who are doing physically demanding work or manual work, and an extra set of hands is needed, be the extra set of hands. Be willing to do whatever it is that you ask others to do. It shows respect and your recognition of the importance of the task.

4. *Work as hard, or harder, than the people under your supervision.*

   This is leading by example, but it is more. It demonstrates your belief in the importance of the objective. It demonstrates your respect for the work performed by others. Negative "leadership" occurs when the person in authority delegates a difficult or unpleasant task then simply waits for someone else to perform.

5. *Treat everyone with the same level of importance and respect, regardless of their jobs.*

Every organization has a structure and a hierarchy of responsibility and authority. There are "bosses" and employees of one sort or another. There is no such hierarchy when it comes to respect. Everyone who does their job conscientiously is entitled to the same level of respect, regardless of the role.

It is a measure of a person to observe how he or she behaves toward those who may not seem to be important to that person's career or life. I have always watched to see if a person treated me, or another partner, with more respect than he or she treated the staff. Acting dismissively of someone whose job is perceived to be less important is a serious character flaw which I would not overlook.

6. *Earn respect.*

A person in a position of responsibly will never be an effective leader without earning the respect of those in his or her charge. You do not get respect by being the boss and having authority over others. You cannot demand respect. You cannot pay for it. You have to *earn* it. You earn respect, in large part, by showing respect to all who are in your charge and by conducting yourself in a way that is worthy of that respect.

7. *Be accessible to your personnel.*

You cannot gain the respect of those who you are leading by remaining distant from them, particularly if you are in a small organization where daily or frequent contact is the norm. You cannot build personal loyalty in a small organization through an intermediary. If you have something to say to one of your people, positive or negative, you must deal with them personally and directly. Direct contact builds trust. Dealing with personnel through an intermediary, when direct communication is readily available, is disrespectful and creates distrust.

Let your personnel know that your door is open to them if they have an issue to discuss or a problem to address. It will not only let your personnel know that their concerns are important, it will make you aware of potential issues and allow you to resolve them before they become larger issues. Most importantly, by dealing with personnel directly, you can deliver your message and resolve issues in a way which is consistent with the values and culture that you are trying to promote.

8. *Let people know when they are performing well, and that their work is both important and appreciated.*

Most people work, in the first instance, to provide for their immediate needs. Next in importance is the pride which they feel knowing that they have done well.

Everyone who works for pay is expected to do the job for which he or she is being paid but not everyone does their job willingly and with enthusiasm. Like respect, you have to earn the enthusiasm of those in your charge by respecting what they do when they do it well. When people know that their good work is respected and appreciated, they feel justifiably proud of what they do. They are more likely to live up to the level of performance and the respect which they have earned. If their good work is taken for granted, there is no motivation to excel.

Everyone appreciates having their efforts recognized. A simple recognition like *"well done* or *"that's a good job. I really appreciate it,"* provided that it is genuine, can mean a great deal to someone who has worked hard on a project. It is a recognition that the effort has not gone unnoticed and is not taken for granted. It is a statement of appreciation for the fact that the person has brought their best to the task and has not simply shown up. It is a sign of respect and a source of pride for the person whose efforts are recognized.

Much of this is common sense, but most of us don't have time to think about the details so I have attempted to express them here. In the end, the simple rule is to have respect for anyone in any job who is doing their best. If you remember that, everything else will follow.

BE A CRITICAL THINKER

*"People want you to be honest,
but only when they agree with you."*

Charles Barkley

I fully expect that most of the people who read these pages are already critical thinkers. I am writing on the subject to encourage some additional thought and to highlight some of the areas that we might tend to overlook critical thinking in our daily lives.

Critical thinking does not mean being cynical, rude or dismissive. It does mean being able to listen to and evaluate, *objectively and respectfully,* opinions and information even when it supports an opposing or unpopular point of view. It means thinking independently, not as part of a group. When you support group thinking you necessarily adopt, at least impliedly, the views of the group.

Most people think of themselves as critical thinkers, and most are, in many respects. Unfortunately, we often tend to apply our critical thinking skills selectively, where it is convenient or interesting to do so, or where it aligns with our pre-conceived views. We can sometimes simply forget to question things that we are told when the source seems authoritative or reliable. In other instances, looking for hard evidence can be both uncomfortable and unpopular. Looking for the objective truth requires a conscious effort and, sometimes, the courage to stand alone.

Finding the truth isn't easy. We are constantly being bombarded with misinformation, half-truths and outright lies---usually in support of someone's personal agenda or pre-conceived point of view. The sources often seem credible. In my years of practicing law I questioned hundreds of witnesses. I have seen many, many, people evade the truth or lie outright, very often under oath and under penalty of perjury. Some just embellished facts or stretched the truth without quite breaking it. Others, and not uncommonly, lied outright. Still others--- and these are the most difficult to detect-- are those who, for one reason or another, truly believe what they are saying even when the irrefutable evidence is to the contrary. In these cases, money was not the motive. I have observed this when people are recounting a highly stressful experience, when the truth is too difficult for them to accept, or when they are so otherwise invested in their belief that it becomes true to them. They are entirely credible, because they *believe* what they are saying even when it is demonstrably wrong. It is far more common than one might expect. It is why, for example, you cannot simply accept, blindly, the reports that you see on the news taken from "eyewitnesses" who seem entirely credible.

Don't rationalize facts to suit your point of view.

I have long been fascinated by how willing the general public seems to be to accept, almost without question, much of what they hear in the form of advertising, gossip, talk show hosts, news commentators, professors, and the like. What is actually shocking to me, however, even after all these years, is that many intelligent people will dismiss or rationalize away hard evidence when the evidence is not what they want to hear.

Unfortunately, all too few people are really interested in the facts, supported by hard evidence, because hard evidence is difficult to dismiss. We all tend to be more willing to accept, as true, what we want to hear. We tend to dismiss or rationalize information that does not agree with our preconceived beliefs or values. This phenomenon explains why commenters have been thriving, more than ever before, by "spinning" the truth and half-truths to their respective audiences. It is why people gravitate to news outlets which will spin the facts to give them the "affirmation" they are looking for rather than information that they need to form an unbiased decision. Audiences know which sources of information will give them a favorable spin on the facts and which will rationalize information which they do not want to hear.

Thinking independently can be unpopular.

The need to think independently is not limited to the political arena or to social commentary. It is at least as important in our personal lives. Our closest friends and acquaintances often share popular opinions on personal or social issues which are socially difficult to challenge. The "knee-jerk" acceptance of currently popular points of view is more the rule than the exception. To disagree with a commonly accepted point of view can be hugely unpopular. There is often a rational opposing point of view to any popularly held belief which should at least be understood and considered, even if not ultimately accepted.

Don't blindly accept the views of "experts"

The same caution applies to opinions of anyone deemed to be "knowledgeable" or an "expert" on a particular subject. This includes credentialed educators or lecturers who may appear to be highly regarded. Having academic or other "credentials" and being in a position to lecture others does not always equate to truth or common sense. Credentials are often acquired without any measure of objectivity, logic, or good sense. This is certainly true in disciplines where there are no concrete or verifiable answers, only philosophies and opinions. Whenever anyone pontificates on a particular point of view, it is wise to consider the underlying basis for the opinion, the thought processes upon which the opinions are based, and whether the person offering the opinion is objective and free of pre-conceptions and biases.

The scientific community is less likely to engage in this kind of "soft" thinking because, generally, scientific and mathematic problems have objective verifiable answers. However, even here, it is wise to question the foundation for opinions that may have consequences. Sometimes the brightest and most objective experts can simply get it wrong. And don't hesitate to ask fundamental questions, just because you may not have the technical expertise.

Over the years, I have worked with some of the most respected and qualified experts in a wide range of disciplines. These included highly qualified people in areas of engineering, finance, psychology, medicine, and a host of other areas. Invariably, these experts had advanced degrees from some of the finest academic institutions. All were highly qualified and highly regarded in their respective fields. I was totally unqualified in those areas of expertise and totally out of my depth.

In each instance, I would have to rely on these experts to provide conclusions and opinions on issues with potentially serious consequences. Each expert would eventually have to defend his or her position under oath. Any weakness or flaw in the expert's analysis and conclusions would be revealed through the crucible of cross-examination. For that reason, I was compelled to challenge the analysis and conclusions of people who were far brighter and who were experts in areas of which I knew little or nothing. On occasion, the challenge would reveal some weakness, some false assumption, which would have weakened or made the conclusions useless.

Whether the expert is a political commentator, a professor, a doctor, or simply a friend, opinions and conclusions are almost always based on (1) assumptions and (2) facts. Even when you are not an expert, you can question the foundations, the assumptions and the facts.

The assumptions can sometimes be influenced by preconceived beliefs. Often those who are publicly regarded as "knowledgeable" in a particular field including professors in the social sciences, philosophy, etc. may have derived their basic beliefs, their basic information and assumptions, from schools and schools of thought that share the same biases. The biases may be compounded by a lack of real world experience. This can be a kind of "intellectual bubble, or a form of "intellectual incest."

Here is one example: I once had a professor from a prominent law school phone to interview me in connection with a paper that he was writing on potential effect which punitive damage laws might have on businesses. When I explained the uncertainty and dangers that the current application of the law was actually having on certain businesses, it was not what he wanted to hear. He told me that it was not what his research showed. I am sure that is what he told his law school class and what he put in his article. But he was dealing with abstract information in a safe and sterile "bubble" of an academic environment. I was dealing with real clients, in real businesses, facing real and unpredictable risks in the real world. [1] Don't blindly accept the experts. Always look at the foundation.

There is often a difference between what we think we "know" and what we "really know."

We need to be sure of our facts on issues that matter. We all rely on information that we "know" to be true in our daily lives without checking the foundation for each and every piece of information. There is no need to check our routine assumptions because most do not have serious consequences. However, when consequences can be serious, such as when it affects the reputation of a friend or acquaintance, it is important to consider the foundation. In that context, we need to distinguish between hard facts and information based upon good faith, but unfounded, beliefs.

---

[1] The abuses and negative effects of punitive damage awards eventually became so critical that the United States Supreme Court, and many states, imposed defined legal standards and limits for awards of punitive damages awards.

I have often had occasion to prepare witnesses who were about to give sworn testimony on a particular issue. The witnesses were presented to me because they "knew" important facts or had some specific knowledge relevant to our case. The witnesses were people who were honest and acting on their good faith belief that they "knew" what they believed they knew. However, when we drilled down to learn the actual source of their knowledge, we often learned that their sincere, good faith, beliefs lacked a solid factual foundation. They may have been relying on what was commonly accepted as true in their workplace or on what they were told by a colleague. Neither is reliable enough to be evidence.

This occurs because we "know" information on different levels. In our day-to-day lives, and in normal conversation, we routinely tell each other things that we "know" because we have heard the information on the news, because it is considered common knowledge, or because we heard it from a reliable source. That kind of information is fine for conversation and is generally reliable enough for our day to day dealings. However, if put to the test, it might not withstand scrutiny. While we do not need to scrutinize every piece of information that we are given, we should scrutinize information that may have real consequences to our lives and to our beliefs.

Always ask "why?"

Finally, always ask "why?" There are almost always two sides to every story, regardless of how obvious a conclusion might seem. We often hear reports, whether in the media, in school, or in our private lives, of some apparently outrageous decision made by a court, a school, or a political body. The decisions are usually presented at face value with no in-depth analysis as to why the decision was made. Ask why.

It is important to know the whole story. No matter how clear the issue seems, there are often missing facts which are essential to a truly informed judgement. I have experienced many instances in which all of the evidence in my possession pointed to just one conclusion. The answer was clear to me. Then, learning just one, or a few, additional facts, I was compelled to reverse the conclusion which I reached earlier. Getting all of the facts and getting both sides of the story matters. There is often some background, some history, some rationale which has not been reported in those instances where the conclusion seems too odd to be true. Always ask why.

I have not written this to create cynicism or to encourage people to be dismissive of everything we hear or to be dismissive of the views of others. My goal is to simply create a level of awareness that, on matters of importance, we should develop a habit of private skepticism, and a willingness to look for the truth, even when it is uncomfortable.

Some tools for determining credibility

There is no way to get to the truth on all issues but there are tools to help in making a better approximation of what is likely to be truthful, and what is not.

As I started to synthesize my own thoughts on this subject, I found myself coming back to many of the criteria used to evaluate the reliability of information before it can be considered as evidence in a court of law.

The information must be (1) relevant to the issue and (2) the information must be *reliable.* Although juries and courts don't always reach the right conclusions, the standards for evaluating *reliability* of admissible evidence has evolved over hundreds of years from the English common law. Those standards makes good sense in law and in life. Here is a layman's thumbnail of some of the things that I consider when deciding what to believe:

1. Is there a reliable foundation for the information?

    * *What is the source of the information?* Is it from personal knowledge, or is someone simply repeating what they had been told or what they read?

    * *Is the information fact or opinion?* Opinions are not a good source of information. (Opinions are *not* routinely allowed in court because they are not evidence and are generally *unreliable.*) [2]

2. *Is the information complete?* Are you hearing or seeing *all* of the information on *both* sides of the issue?

    * Can the information be verified objectively-- or is the information someone else's editing of the information or interpretation of the facts?

---

[2] There is an exception which allows opinion testimony where scientific or technical expertise is required and where the court determines, in advance, that the procedure used to explain a technical issue is commonly accepted in that field and has been subject to peer review.

3. More importantly, is the person providing the information reliable and objective:

- Does the person providing the information have *personal knowledge of the facts* or is the information derived from another person or other sources, which means the facts have been subject to editing, interpretation, opinion, and, potentially, bias?

  Statements or opinions based on what others have said or written is hearsay. It is inherently untrustworthy because there is no opportunity to question or challenge the foundation, completeness, or accuracy of the information.

- Does the person who is providing information have a *history of truthfulness and accuracy*—Does the person have a history of being accurate, objective, and unbiased?

- Does the person have a demonstrated willingness to accept opposing views where it is justified by the evidence?

- Most importantly, does the person providing the information have a *potential bias or motive* to spin the information toward or against a particular point of view?

If you apply these standards, you will see why most news reports should be viewed with caution and why professional commentators should be rejected outright as a reliable source of information.

News Reports: News reports are a valuable way to keep abreast of current issues, and foster debate, but they cannot be relied upon as accurate and complete sources of information. Even the most professional and objective news outlets necessarily have to edit the news to decide what portion of the story you will see and hear. News outlets need to rely on information provided by others who may be biased or unreliable. Sometimes, the information is provided by "eyewitnesses" who are, often, unreliable. New reports are almost never allowed in evidence because they are unreliable and hearsay. There is no opportunity to question the validity of the information that they provide.

Also, many media outlets simply have a political bias. [3]

Commentators: Political commentators and philosophical and social lecturers are among the worst sources of factual information. They can provide food for debate but are virtually useless as a source of complete, accurate, objective, and reliable information:

People who make their living opining on political and social issues often do not have personal knowledge of the "facts" which support their opinions. Instead, they tend to rely on what they have been told or have read--often from sources that support their pre-conceived point of view.

Professional commentators almost always have a political, social, or philosophical bias which slants their

---

[3] Notice that news reports thrive on the negative and the cynical. They are cynical in the sense that they almost always ascribe some ulterior motive to every decision made by a court or public figure. While cynicism is often justified, we should not assume that every decision has a cynical motive. Sometimes people sometimes do things just because they believe it is the right thing to do. That is often the case with highly publicized court decisions.

conclusions. It is how they earn their living. Wherever there is an inherent bias, truth and accuracy will suffer.

Professional commentators have a second, powerful, motive to rationalize and skew their opinions. Professional commentators usually thrive preaching to specific audiences, with specific points of view. Those audiences tune in to particular commentators to have their pre conceived views affirmed. Commentators pandering to an audience with one point of view will not survive long by taking a contrary point of view.

Never trust anyone who always tells you what you want to hear. Distrust any source which always agrees with your point of view. Distrust any source which never concedes the opposing point of view. Distrust any source which claims to have all the answers.

I have focused on the news media and professional commentators because we are surrounded by the information which they provide daily and that information is often incomplete at best or intentionally misleading at worst. However, the principles of quiet skepticism should apply to all forms of rumor and gossip that we experience in our personal lives.

Rumor and gossip is almost always incomplete or inaccurate on key facts, and often biased. Remember, there are almost always two sides to every issue. Get all the facts. This is particularly important where the reputation of a colleague or friend is at stake.

Truth really matters. If you can't defend your point of view with the truth, you have the wrong point of view. Sometimes the truth may cut against your position or hurt your side of the issue. Don't move the goalposts, don't change your standards, just because the evidence cuts against your personal point of view. If your point of view is correct, your position becomes stronger and more credible when you can prove your point while still acknowledging the facts which may work against you.

IN THE WORKPLACE

Look them in the eye and give them a firm handshake.

Roy Silane

There are certain basic, common sense, practices which, over time, will all but guarantee that you will be a success in the workplace or with any organization with which you are associated. These basic common sense practices are far rarer in the real world than you might think. If you practice them reliably, you will become a valuable asset to any organization.

In simplest terms, you should consider the qualities that you would want to have in an ideal employee or colleague if you were making the decision.

When I was hiring or evaluating someone, I always looked, first, at whether the person would likely be a loyal, positive member of the team. I looked for a positive attitude, reliability, honesty, and someone who sought to solve problems, not create them. I tried to avoid individuals who were quick to complain, who did not get along, who brought their personal issues to work. I tried to avoid anyone that I could not count on when I needed them. It sounds like common sense, and it is, but to find someone who exhibits these qualities, consistently, is relatively rare.

There are occasions where someone will get an immediate sense of your qualities based on a single meeting or interview. You only have one chance to make a good first impression. My father preached a simple rule when meeting someone for the first time—*"Look them in the eye and give them a firm handshake."* When you look someone in the eye and give a firm handshake, you show your interest in and respect for the person you are meeting and you demonstrate confidence in yourself. Respect and confidence are two qualities that you want to project.

Here are some of the other qualities and habits that are highly regarded in any organization:

1. *A positive attitude:*

   A positive attitude is critically important. The only truly unforgivable sin is a bad attitude. A person who works diligently but makes a mistake should be forgiven. A person who doesn't care won't be forgiven.

   Maintaining a positive attitude helps produce positive results, motivates others, and is an asset to any organization. Anything less than a positive attitude is a negative attitude and is a problem.

2. *100 percent reliability, not 98 percent:*

   If you want to be truly valuable you need to be there (1) whenever you are expected to be there and (2) whenever you are needed. People need to know that they can count on you. If you are unreliable, even some of the time, they will not know for sure that they can rely on you when they need you. People who are always reliable are valued and appreciated.

3. *Look for solutions, don't bring problems:*

   The last thing any organization needs is more problems. Whatever your job, you are there to solve problems, not make them. Avoid any behavior or involvement which makes life more difficult for your superiors or those around you.

Don't get involved in office politics or personal issues. Those kinds of issues create problems which you need to avoid.

If you are confronted with a work-related challenge, try to find a solution or positive suggestion, if at all possible.

4. *Don't bring personal problems to work:*

Everyone has personal issues. Keep them out of the workplace if at all possible.

5. *Be loyal:*

Being loyal is associated with having a positive attitude and with being reliable. No one wants to be around anyone who is not committed to the work they are doing. Even if you are unhappy with your work, or plan to change jobs, be loyal to what you are doing for as long as you are doing it. It is a mark of character which will earn respect and pay dividends.

6. *Be on time—all the time:*

Being late is being disrespectful. It sends a message of disregard for whomever you are scheduled to meet.

In the work environment, if you are just on time for a meeting or commitment, you are already late. Being five minutes early, all the time, sends a message of respect.

7. *Be enthusiastic and energetic:*

Energy and enthusiasm are important qualities in the workplace for two important reasons.

First, you will only do your best, and achieve the best results, if you are eager to do the work that you are doing.

Secondly, energy and enthusiasm sends the right message. Those qualities are recognized as part of an overall positive attitude, of a diligent worker, and a team player. They are qualities that are common to most successful people.

The reverse can give the appearance of indifference.

It may be difficult to be energetic and enthusiastic if you find yourself in a position which is somewhat routine or boring. It is important to make the effort to be energetic in your work regardless of how you feel about the work. It is a valuable habit and a good reflection of your character. It will also reflect on your personal reputation which will follow you.

8. *Under promise—over deliver:*

Disappointment occurs when someone fails to live up to expectations. If the expectation is set high, the performance must be equally high to avoid disappointment. If the expectation is kept within reason, anything which exceeds expectation will be seen as a positive. Manage expectations by under promising—then deliver more than was expected.

9. *Never assume:*

It is common for people to make mistakes based on assumptions which turn out to be unjustified or incorrect. When that happens you might hear the person involved explaining why the assumption was perfectly reasonable. There is no such thing as a "reasonable" assumption when the facts really matter. When facts really matter, you need to confirm the facts before you can reasonably rely on them.

10. *Dress for success:*

No one will ever say it outright, but appearance matters. Regardless of what others in the organization say or do, look your best. Dress consistently with whatever dress code applies but dress, within that code, as presentably as possible.

Do not indulge in faddish styles, bling, or anything which would cause your appearance to bring undue attention to yourself. People won't generally tell you what looks inappropriate but they will think it.

If you follow these simple rules, consistently, you will be valuable to any organization with which you are associated. You will eventually be successful. It may take time and patience but these are timeless qualities that any employer or organization will value and respect.

KEEP YOUR LIFE SIMPLE

When you arise in the morning, give thanks for the food and for the joy of living. If you see no reason to give thanks, the fault lies only in yourself. . . Show respect to all people and grovel to none.

Chief Tecumseh

(Shawnee Chief and Warrior)

Leading a happy and productive life is actually very simple. We complicate it when we make unwise or bad choices. Don't complicate your life.

Every day, we hear some life "expert" who presents him or herself as an expert on how to live. Now, and in every generation in my lifetime, there are people earning their living with books, seminars, and public appearances who purport to have divined the latest formula to make our problems disappear. Unfortunately, there are no newly discovered "silver bullets" on how to live. The proclaimed "experts," and the fads, come and go in every generation.

The formula for a stable happy life is timeless and is really very simple. Set your standards and principles and stand by them. Don't complicate your life by avoiding your own principles when it seems expedient to do so. Adhering to basic principles will not insulate you from life's trials and tragedies, but it will equip you to deal with them. Adhering to basic principles *will* prevent you from complicating your life and will prevent you from compounding the issues that all of us must face. It will avoid adding unnecessary stresses to your life. Perhaps most importantly, it will give you self-respect and personal peace of mind.

Here is my very basic—and admittedly very simplistic—checklist for how we should try to live:

1. Each day, set out to do your best at whatever you have to do.
2. Try to do the right things, even when it seems painful.
3. Respect everyone
4. Be of service to others
5. Stand up to the bullies.
6. Go to bed and be at peace.

I know—I know!-- this appears to be a gross oversimplification. But, if you take a moment to think about it and break it apart, it really makes uncomplicated sense. It is a timeless and easy to remember blueprint for how to live your life. If you do nothing more, you will be fine.

People complicate their lives by making bad choices. The bad choices may be in the selection of friends, seeking immediate gratification, in the way we deal with personal relationships, being ambitious to the point that we compromise our principles, and a thousand other possible excesses. We can avoid those excesses, and avoid the choices which complicate our lives by: (1) setting clear principles for ourselves and (2) deciding—*before* any issue arises—that we will not abandon those principles, even when the consequences will seem to be painful. If we are committed to our principles before an issue arises, we don't have to ponder, and possibly weaken, when the pressure of the moment arises. If we set the ground rules for ourselves, and stay within them, we will never go far wrong.

The reverse is true. Compromising principles are a slippery slope. The first misstep often complicates the issue, and leads to other bad decisions. The "rule of holes" applies here. The "rule of holes" is "*When you are already in a hole, stop digging.*" In simple terms, when you have screwed up, face it. Don't make the situation worse by compromising your principles to seek the easy way out, which often leads you deeper into the hole.

Let me elaborate on each of the points in my simplistic checklist:

1. *Each day, set out to do your best at whatever you have to do.*

   Regardless of age or position in life, we each have duties and responsibilities. The responsibilities may be challenging, interesting, and rewarding, or they may be unfulfilling and boring. What matters is doing your best at whatever you are called to do. If you have a habit of always trying to do your best, you will never go far wrong. You will earn respect and you will have far fewer regrets, even when things don't work out.

   The admonition to "do your best" is something that most of us hear from early childhood—so much so that we probably don't reflect on why we should do our best or the consequences of not doing our best. So here are some thoughts on why this basic idea is so important to the simple life formula:

Doing your best is always worthy of respect. Halfhearted efforts are not. It is a lesson that I learned, repeatedly, from my father. I often observed his respect and admiration for anyone who he saw doing their job well and especially when someone with a menial or less rewarding job took pride in their work. Most of us respect, instinctively, anyone who works hard and does their job well and with pride, regardless of their station in life. The reverse is also true. No one respects a shirker or a person that does the minimum, just to get by.

Doing your best, even when the work is menial and no one is looking, is evidence of character and character matters. As I write this, I am reminded of my own instinctive response to a young, quiet sailor who, at the time, had a lower end and unglamorous job where he was not subject to direct supervision. Every time I would look in on that sailor, he would be doing his job enthusiastically and with a positive attitude, and never with a complaint. He worked that way when no one was looking. I couldn't help but respect this modest, quiet, sailor's character.

Later, the sailor got in some trouble while off duty. With a few drinks, on a cold Philadelphia night, he decided to "borrow" a rental car which someone had left with the motor running. He drove the car into the hands of the police a block away. Knowing his character, I was more than anxious to speak on his behalf – (and with the enthusiastic support and blessing of our ship's Captain who also recognized his qualities). When I appeared with him in court, I saw that my estimate of his character was not misplaced.

The same police who arrested him were also there and were also eager to put in a good word for him --as did the owner of the car. They described him as respectful and polite. Character matters, and doing your best all the time is one sign of character. It's like putting money in the bank for the time that you need to make a "withdrawal" –when you need to rely on your reputation. The judge dismissed the case.

Putting our best effort into any task is also a source of self-satisfaction, personal pride and, equally important, peace of mind. Of course, our best effort gives us the best chance of succeeding at whatever we set out to do, but it is also a source of comfort and peace of mind when our best effort just isn't enough.

To fail, without knowing that we have tried our best is deflating and demoralizing. The reverse is also true. There is a certain peace of mind that comes with being able to say to yourself, truthfully, "Well I have done my best."

2. *Try to do the right things.*

I have observed that doing what is right, even when it is painful, simplifies the issues, earns respect, and gives peace of mind. The more good you do, the better your life will be.

Taking shortcuts, avoiding the truth when it is painful to admit the truth, dishonesty, disloyalty, unbridled ambition, greed, etc. invariably complicate lives and the complications usually result in stress and unhappiness.

Sometimes it is not easy to know what the "right" choice may be, particularly when we *really* want to do something. In simple terms, that answer lies within each of us. There is a lawyer who has worked against me in many cases but whom I have come to respect and know as a friend because of his unfailing integrity. His rule of thumb, when determining the "right" thing to do is the "cringe test." Simply put, if a possible course of conduct makes you instinctively "cringe," it is probably the wrong thing to do. The "cringe test" assumes that you have a basic understanding of right and wrong, as most people do. It's called a "conscience." We can be tempted to rationalize a decision which we know, instinctively, is wrong simply because it is what we want to do. But you can't hide from yourself. If it feels wrong, if it makes you uncomfortable, it probably is wrong.

If you "keep it simple" by following your conscience, and doing the right thing, you will avoid most of the complications that have negative consequences. And you will earn peace of mind.

The concept that following a good conscience leads to a fulfilled life is not mine and it is certainly is not new. Minds far greater than mine have advanced this view, one way or another, for centuries. Aristotle believed that happiness is the reward for works of virtue. His ideas were incorporated into the thirteenth century philosophy of Thomas Aquinas who provided the foundation for four hundred and fifty years of Jesuit education in universities throughout the world to this day. It is inferred in the words of Chief

Tecumseh, cited above. It is foundational to all of the great religions of the world. It just makes sense.

You need only look at the news each day to see people who, one way or another, have complicated their lives and brought unhappiness on themselves by taking short cuts, pursuing selfish ends, or making other bad choices. Keep life simple by being true to your principles and values. It will not only earn you respect and admiration, it will allow you to sleep at night.

3. *Respect Everyone.*

Everyone should be treated with respect, unless and until they prove otherwise. Everyone is entitled to be treated with respect, regardless of their station in life. Everyone should be respected for who they are not what they are.

A person's station in life has nothing to do with whether they are worthy of respect. Be impressed with how people lead their lives and not with their perceived level of importance. There is no such thing as an "important" person. People are sometimes called upon to do important jobs, or take on the important responsibilities. They may have importance as long as they are doing the important job, but no job lasts forever. No one is irreplaceable. When they are finished with their important job, when their years of fame and fortune have passed, they are just who they are, just like everyone else. Their residual value is measured by who they are as a person, when they no longer have an important job, fame, or fortune.

On a personal note, there is one trait that I have observed -- fortunately very infrequently--and which I have found to be a serious character flaw. On occasion, I have observed someone in the work environment treating senior personnel with deference and respect, while being dismissive, or worse, to the working staff. To me that is the professional "kiss of death." It is an unfortunate statement of the person's true character. In many instances, it may actually be the member of the staff that is truly worthy of respect.

Treat everyone with respect, genuinely. If a person is unworthy of respect, you will know it in due course.

4. *Be of service to others.*

In the very broadest of terms, people can be divided into two categories: those who care only (or primarily) for themselves and those who also care for other people. You need to be in the second group.

Being of service to others doesn't just assist others. It provides purpose and meaning for your life.

This concept does not require you to devote your time to some specific cause or duty. It does mean that, whatever you do in life, you should be ready lend a hand to someone who needs help when you reasonably can. The opportunities present themselves in countless ways in our daily lives, with friends, relatives, colleagues, bosses, employees, etc. The helping hand can be as elaborate as you want it to be or may be as simple as providing moral support to a friend or colleague. It is simply a matter of helping where you can.

I stumbled upon what is purported to be an old Chinese proverb. Maybe it is and maybe it isn't, but it is worth repeating:

If you want happiness for an hour — take a nap.
If you want happiness for a day — go fishing.
If you want happiness for a year — inherit a fortune.
If you want happiness for a lifetime — help someone.

If you (1) always do your best; (2) try to do the right things; (3) treat everyone with respect; (stand up when the need arises and (4) and try to be of service to others, you will keep your life simple, you will never go far wrong. Unfortunately, not everyone "plays nice." Which leads to the last element of our simple formula:

5. *Stand up to the bullies.*

There are times when you simply must stand up and be counted. It does not mean fighting every issue. It does mean standing firm, even under pressure, when it matters-- in support of someone who needs your help, in support of what you believe is right, or when you need to defend an important principal.

The five steps which I have discussed are broad guidelines which, to my observations, have defined the people who have led quality lives and who have earned my respect. If you make an effort each day to live within those guidelines, you will likely reach the last step:

6. *Go to bed, feel good about yourself, and be at peace.*

COMMUNICATION SKILLS

It's not enough to say something,
You have to be understood.

The ability to communicate effectively, both orally and in writing, is an essential skill for anyone who aspires to be in a top leadership position. This is easy to see. You will notice that every leader in every field of endeavor has the ability to communicate well. It is true of political leaders, military leaders, leaders in the field of medicine, revolutionaries, or religious leaders. The one thing that the leaders in each field have in common is the ability to communicate.

The essential practical point here is contained in the statement which I have put at the top of the page: *It is not enough to say something. You have to be understood.* While this may seem to be a simple common sense idea, it is remarkable how often it is ignored.

There is one small practical example that I find particularly annoying. In my experience, it is common for someone to leave a telephone voice message in which the person calling speaks slowly and clearly to leave a message requiring a call back. Then the caller, having now delivered the message, rushes through the very end of the call with the voice trailing off, leaving the return telephone number that is almost unintelligible: " **CALL ME** back at 777 212 1234." Perhaps the most important part of the message was the return telephone number, yet it is often the most difficult to understand. It's a small example of the importance of not just saying something, but making sure that you are understood.

Always follow up

I have observed situations in which a person is criticized for not passing on some important piece of information. The person then defends him or herself by saying "I told you . . ." or " I put that in an e-mail." Those responses simply aren't good enough. Were they understood?

When you have to pass along information, you need to make sure that the information is *recognized* and *understood.* You are not excused from that obligation by being able to say that you actually passed along that information, either verbally, or in an email. To satisfy your obligation to be understood, you need to make sure that the person who is to receive the information: (1) heard the information; or (2) read the email; and (3) acknowledged in some way that they understood what was communicated. If you follow that simple rule, you will avoid miscommunications and the problems which usually follow.

Public Speaking

There is a tactic among trial lawyers that, when you need to get a point across to a jury, you need to repeat the point again and again. It's not because trial lawyers think that juries are incapable of understanding. It is because they recognize that key information, key details, can be lost among all of the other words and information being presented to the jury. If you listen to really good public speakers, you will notice that they have the ability to make sure that the key points are not lost among all of their other comments.

Let me try a hypothetical example: Let's assume I am delivering a presentation to explain agricultural production. I can say *"Productivity in this area has been very high notwithstanding the recent drought with 222 pounds of potatoes per acre, 422 pounds of rutabaga 332 pounds of carrots, totaling to 1,620 pounds of produce in an area usually limited 932 pounds of produce."*

If I simply carried on from there, what do you think the chance would be that the audience would be able to tell me how many pounds of rutabaga were grown or precisely how this year's production compared with previous years? Probably not very good.

If you wanted the audience to really get the data, you might say: *". . . 222 pounds of potatoes per acre--that's 222 pounds of potatoes; 422 pounds of rutabaga--that's just rutabaga--422 pounds; and 332 pounds of carrots— 332 pounds of carrots. All of which comes to a total— and this is the important point—the total this year is 1,620 pounds of produce compared to a prior average of 932 pounds of produce.*

This is a somewhat boring example but it is a boring subject. If you want people to listen where you are providing boring data, and you want them to get the data correctly, you need to slow down and repeat the important data, so that it is not missed. If you just roll through the data and carry on, most of it will be lost.

The same is true on any important point that you want to make. It helps the audience to tell them what is important: *"the important point here is . . . "* or *"the reason this information is important is . . . "* or something similar. You are telling an audience which may be filled with halfhearted listeners that something important is coming and that they need to pay closer attention. If the point is important, you can explain the point then say it again in different words: *"To put it differently . . . . "*

These are just random examples intended to highlight the issue.

The essential issue is that it can be useless to simply say something. You have to make sure that it was heard, recognized and understood. If you keep that rule in mind, you will come up with your own style and your own way of making sure that you are communicating effectively.

DON'T PUT OFF DEALING WITH ISSUES

"The only difference between success and failure is the ability to take action."

Alexander Graham Bell

When you have something to do, or when you have some follow up to accomplish, don't delay—do it promptly.

There are at least two good reasons to stay ahead of even routine issues.

The first reason is that issues, even small ones, accumulate. The stresses that go along with addressing issues also accumulate. The more things you have to do, the more likely you will be to make a mistake and the more likely you will add, unnecessarily, to your level of stress.

Issues don't get better with age. If you deal with every issue promptly, you will accomplish more, you will be in firmer control of your life, you will have fewer mistakes and regrets, and you will have less stress.

The second reason for dealing with issues promptly is equally important. Many issues may be time sensitive, when they do not appear to be. Issues can become stale when not addressed promptly. We may tend to think that an issue is not time sensitive just because there is no set deadline for dealing with the issue. That can be a very false sense of security.

Issues can become stale and mistakes much harder to correct if you do not get on them promptly.

If someone else has made a mistake which affects you, you need to get on it as soon as possible. If you don't, the problem can be far more difficult to correct. The information needed to correct the error can become stale or missing, the relevant history can be impossible to reconstruct and—this can be important--you lose the sense of urgency that spurs people to action. Instinctively, the issue will not seem to be urgent to the person who has to resolve it if you have not treated it urgently yourself.

Staying on top of issues, large and small–and promptly— is part of keeping your life simple, in control, and stress free.

LOOK FOR THE GOOD

"Be a light, not a judge. Be a model not a critic"[4]

Steven R. Covey

If you set out to look for something negative, you will find it. Don't be that person. Look for the good.

There is no great leader in any field of endeavor who did not make mistakes and who did not have flaws. There is no society, no government, and no religion, that does not have flaws and abuses in its history that it would like to change. We need to look at the totality of the individual life and the totality of the organization to determine its value, just as we would want someone to judge us on the totality of our lives rather than judging us only on the basis of our mistakes.

All people, even the greatest among us, have human weaknesses and failings. But some have served great causes, made great personal sacrifices and have performed great service to humanity despite their shortcomings and mistakes. To focus on the mistakes is not only unjust but deprives us of some of the most important lessons and examples of human history.

The same is true of any organization. All governments, religions, and societies have some dark history. Their failings are often not inherent in the ideals of the organizations themselves but are often the product of the misguided people who lead them. Organizations don't cause abuses. People cause abuses. If the goals and objectives of the organization are meaningful, the goals

---

[4] *"The 7 Habits Of Highly Effective People,"* Steven R. Covey

and objectives do not lose their value because of the people who corrupt them.

We are constantly assaulted by cynical or negative opinions of our institutions and our beliefs. This is not new. There has always been the negative element of society who gets up in the morning with the attitude *"What shall I be against today?"* It has always been profitable for some elements of the media to emphasize controversy. Political commentators and college professors often opine on all that is--or has been--wrong in society and its institutions according to their personal biases. But how many have focused the positives? How many have balanced the criticisms with the achievements, focused on those countless people who have sacrificed for others and sacrificed for the highest ideals of society? Not many. Beware of the critics with personal agendas.

I do not suggest that we should dismiss or turn a blind eye to all that is wrong now or in our history. We must look at those issues openly to correct what we can now to learn from the errors of the past.

My objective here is simply to avoid the trap of just being a critic. It is easy to be cynical and to criticize, particularly when we are not the ones being judged. But we need to look at the whole picture. We need to be aware of and appreciate the positive and achievements of those who have sacrificed greatly, maybe imperfectly, for high ideals and for the blessings that we enjoy. We should judge individuals on the totality of how they live their lives and what they contributed to society, and not just on the basis of their mistakes and shortcomings. We need to judge institutions on the basis of values, goals, objectives and achievements and not only on the basis of human shortcomings and mistakes of their members.

I have found it to be valuable to read biographies of people who stood on principle were willing to sacrifice themselves for their principles and for the greater good. Reading about such people helps us to see the side of humanity that is often lost among all of the negative and cynical philosophies and opinions.

Two good places to start are *Profiles in Courage* by John F. Kennedy and *Character is Destiny,* by John McCain. Both are collections short biographies and essays on what it means to have character. [5]

---

[5] John McCain's book is particularly useful because it includes a very diverse selection of both historic and contemporary figures, some of whom are ordinary people who did extraordinary and inspiring things in relative obscurity. One of those ordinary people was one of John McCain's prison guards in a North Vietnamese POW camp.

AFTERWARD

When I started to write this, I wasn't sure how it would develop. I started by selecting topics that I knew were significant, and attempted to write what I knew on each topic separately. As I put them together, it became apparent that each of these topics overlap in one way or another and have several common threads.

In each topic, I found myself using words that were common to the others. The most prominent was the word "respect." It applied in the context of respect for others, in the context of earning respect from others, and in the context of respect for yourself. If you achieve these, you will also have a measure of the other common thread: personal peace of mind.